Ernie's Mindful Journey

Written and illustrated by
Kirsty Topley

Sweet Cherry

Hello, I'm Ernie.

My brain goes

TOO FAST.

I feel like I'm running on a hamster wheel that never **EVER** stops!

It feels like everyone is calm ...

... except me.

'Bernie, how are you always so calm?'

'I'm not always calm, Ernie.
I use mindfulness to help me.'

‘What’s mindfulness?’ asked Ernie.

‘I’LL SHOW YOU!’

'Mindfulness is paying full attention to where you are and what you're doing,' said Bernie.

'Whether you're stretching up high to the bees in the sky.'

'Chasing autumn leaves blowing in the breeze.'

'Or floating along while singing a song.'

'Do something nice, would be my advice.'

'Touch,

taste,

smell,

hear

and see.'

'You'll feel so much calmer when you start to just BE.'

'It might slow your brain
if you dance in the rain.'

‘Or simply do nothing – it’s up to you!’

'So what is it that YOU want to do?'
asked Bernie.

'For now,' said Ernie. 'I want to fish!'

‘After fishing, who knows?’